THE LITTLE
Good Behaviour Guide

Charlotte Preston, RHV, RGN   Trevor Dunton

For Alfie, Sophie, Tilly, Theo, Emilio and Sofia

First published in Great Britain in 1998 by Metro Books
(an imprint of Metro Publishing Limited), 19 Gerrard Street, London W1V 7LA

Text © 1998 Charlotte Preston and Trevor Dunton
Illustrations © 1998 Trevor Dunton

Charlotte Preston and Trevor Dunton are hereby identified as the authors of this work in
accordance with Section 77 of the Copyright, Designs and Patents Act 1988.

British Library Cataloguing in Publication Data.
A CIP record of this book is available on request from the British Library.

ISBN 1 900512 25 4

10 9 8 7 6 5 4 3 2 1

Designed by Mick Keates
Typesetting and formatting by Concise Artisans
Printed in Italy by LEGO

An extra bit for parents with daughters
You'll find that throughout the Little Terror books we refer to babies as 'he'.
Please don't think we've neglected your daughters, it's purely in the interests of clarity and
space. Using he/she, him/her, himself/herself is cumbersome to read and uses valuable space
that we wanted to devote to more useful topics. So, please read 'she' for 'he'.

CONTENTS

This book is about helping you work with your Little Terror to create a happy, loving home. You'll learn what to expect and how to respond. The advice is practical and down-to-earth, with the emphasis on encouragement. The aim is to give you the confidence to deal with any problems that might arise.

Having a child is a bit like being hit on the head by a falling elephant... nothing in life can quite prepare you for it. Your relationship with Little Terror can, of course, bring wonderful rewards, but you can be sure that there will also be challenging moments!

TEACHING GOOD BEHAVIOUR

Bad behaviour or curiosity

Children are born scientists, always experimenting and learning about the world they live in. To make sure that you don't discourage this healthy curiosity, it's important to distinguish between wilful bad behaviour and times when they're simply trying things out and testing boundaries. Hopefully, this book will give you some pointers.

What is good behaviour?

Your idea of 'good' or 'bad' behaviour is not
necessarily the same as someone else's –
even your partner's. Some people might
be driven mad by LT making a mess,
others might see it as creativity.
If one parent was brought up in
a strict household and the other
in a more liberal one, they may
find themselves disagreeing
about how LT should behave.
As you'll see later in the 'Fair
Rules' section, it's important to
sort this out as early as possible
to give LT a clear idea of where
the boundaries are.

Some important things to remember:

1 All babies and children (like their parents) are little terrors some of the time. It's part of growing up.

2 All parents worry about discipline and whether they're 'getting it right'.

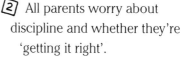

Try to iron out your differences in advance

What makes a difference?

As long as LT is healthy and your expectations are realistic, his behaviour, good or bad, will depend on two things.

Nature: every child is born with a unique personality. This affects the way he responds to the world and makes him who he is. Second-time parents are often amazed at just how different their new baby is from the first one.

Environment: all babies and children learn behaviour from their surroundings and experiences. This means that you have an important effect on Little Terror's behaviour by the way you react to him.

The four basic ingredients:

1. Love
2. Safety
3. Fair rules
4. Healthy diet

Whatever your situation and LT's temperament, as long as you can provide these four things, you'll be giving him every opportunity to grow into a strong, happy, healthy child.

11

Love

This is the most important part of learning. In the beginning, LT's only way of communicating with you is to cry. If he's wet, hungry or miserable, that's all he can do. If you respond to him quickly and give him loads of cuddles, he'll feel secure, knowing that his needs will be met, you're listening and he's loved.

Love builds LT's confidence and self-esteem. He learns by watching and imitating you and will be taking in everything that's going on around him. Even as a newborn baby he can imitate you, for example, poking out your tongue, so if you are loving, he'll learn how to love. If you shout, he'll shout. He thinks you're fantastic and wants to be just like you. He also needs your approval – so give him loads of cuddles and don't pressure him with too many expectations.

Safety

When LT starts playing on his own, cover or remove potential dangers in the room. These include open sockets, wires or cables, sharp-edged furniture, glass and other ornaments.

Fair Rules

Fair Rules are about letting LT know what you can expect from each other. Think about discipline as early as possible so you can start as you mean to go on. LT will understand rules more easily if his carers work as a team. Try to be consistent and strike a balance: too strict and he might become inhibited, uncooperative, or scared to show initiative; too laid back, and he may get out of control.

Putting Fair Rules into practice
Below are some examples of Fair Rules as applied to the topic
of sweets:

 Be consistent
Don't give sweets at the supermarket checkout most days, then say
no when Gran comes with you.

 Be reasonable
Don't put sweets on a table near a three-year-old and then expect
him not to want to eat them.

☆ Mean it (1)

Avoid unrealistic, sweeping statements such as 'You'll never have another sweet if you are naughty' or 'I'll tell your Dad when he comes home, and he'll stop your sweets for ever'.

☆ Mean it (2)

If you say only one sweet, don't give more because he pesters you. This teaches him to disobey.

☆ Be understanding and loving

If you've told him no sweets and he eats one you mistakenly left lying around, let him know that you realise it must have been too hard to resist and give him a hug. He'll learn a lot if you admit you made a mistake.

☆ Give clear, simple instructions

'You can have two sweets when you have finished all your lunch.'

☆ Don't nag; he'll stop listening

'I've told you again and again, no more sweets if you carry on.'

☆ Don't run him down to others, in front of him

'He's terrible, he never stops eating sweets.'

☆ Respect his point of view and involve him in decisions

'What do you think about lots of sweets on Saturdays, and none the rest of the week?'

☆ Punishments should be immediate and in proportion, then forgotten. Show LT he's still loved

'You took Granny's box of chocolates and ate them all. No sweets for you for a week and you'll have to buy Granny another box of chocolates out of your pocket money. Say you are sorry to Granny.' (See page 61 on discipline.)

Of course, most 'Fair Rules' are common sense. It will take patience and understanding to get the balance right.

Give yourselves a break

Get a babysitter and go out together. Remember you had a life before LT! If you're happy, he'll be happy.

Healthy diet

A healthy diet is fundamental to LT's development, and it doesn't have to be expensive or complicated. For advice about diet, please refer to *The Little Terror Good Feeding Guide*. This book covers the behaviour side of eating, forming good eating habits, enjoying mealtimes and developing a healthy attitude to food.

PLAY

Play is an important time when LT can have fun, practise his new skills and try out your Fair Rules. Unless they are ill or unhappy, all children love playing. Try to anticipate LT's changing needs so that the toys and activities you give him are right for his age. Time spent playing with LT is an investment in him and never wasted. At first, LT will need to be shown how to play with things, but he'll also want to experiment and make discoveries for himself. You don't need to play with him all the time: you can be doing the washing up or cooking while he plays; as long as you show an interest and comment on what he's doing.

Playtime tips

Curiosity – As a baby/toddler, LT will want
to explore anything and everything
and experiment with it. With no real
concept of danger or right and
wrong, things are bound to happen.
So, when he fills your CD system
with water, count to ten and try to
remember that curiosity is his way
of learning
about the
world. This is
where 'Fair
Rules' (see
page 14) can
help. If you use
them from the
start and teach
LT what is

acceptable to you, you'll be able to explain to him what he's done wrong without it being a big issue and without too much loss of face on his part.

Praise and encourage LT when he's playing nicely, and try to ignore him when he's being a pain.

Find some friends for LT to play with so that he learns to mix with the outside world, and builds confidence for when he goes to playgroups later on.

Make play interesting – show him things to do, to look at and to think about.

Encourage him to be active – as a baby, he'll enjoy kicking with his nappy off, and when he grows into a toddler, take him to let off steam in the park where he can jump, climb and run around like crazy. Swimming and baby gyms are great from the start.

Let him be leader – it's easy to get into the habit of telling LT what to do. Spend some time every day where he chooses what to do and takes the initiative.

It may seem strange at first, but stick at it and you'll both find it very rewarding. You can use this sort of play to change behaviour patterns, if you're having problems (see page 58).

Let LT take the lead

23

POTTY TRAINING

It might seem like he'll never get the hang of it but he will – when he's ready! Don't let your family and friends pressurise you into starting too early and don't believe Ms Knowitall when she tells you her nephew was dry at one year.

It is not until eighteen months to two years that LT's nervous system will be developed enough to know when he wants to go. By the time he's two, only half of his friends will be dry during the day, but by age three, nine out of ten in the playgroup will be dry most days and six or seven of them will be dry at nights as well. With a bit of luck, LT will be amongst the early ones, but if he isn't, don't worry; by five most children are dry day and night.

Potty training is an important milestone and you can help make the move out of nappies by being relaxed about it, consistent in the training, and by giving him loads of praise. Peeing in the potty nearly always happens first. Pooing comes later. Start when LT has been dry for about two hours, or when he has given you some big hints that he's feeling ready to start such as:

☆ He will start to be aware of a wet or dirty nappy.

☆ He'll know when he's peeing, and will often tell you.

☆ He'll begin to tell you when he's about to pee.

He'll start telling you when he wants to go

Potty training tips

⭐ Show LT the potty – tell him what it is for and leave it around the house. Try him on a child's toilet seat. It will help if you let him see you using the toilet.

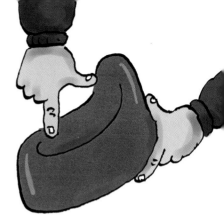

⭐ If he poos at the same time each day – take his nappy off and let him try the potty. If he doesn't like it, put the nappy back on and leave it for a week or two. Give him lots of praise for performing or just for sitting there. (no need for rewards – if he's ready, he'll want to use the potty).

⭐ Get LT to sit on the pot at regular times – like after meals and drinks, before and after his bath, first thing in the morning and last thing at night.

⭐ **Leave the nappy off** – you can use towelling trainer pants; otherwise just carry plenty of spares, and buy some absorbent sheets for the bed in case of accidents.

⭐ **If possible, start in the summer** – LT will be wearing fewer clothes, and he can run around outside without pants.

⭐ **Carry spares** – a nappy and a set of clothes in case of accidents.

⭐ **Accidents will happen** – so keep cool and don't show you're cross. He hasn't done it on purpose!

Though it can seem to be taking ages, stick with it and don't worry about other LTs getting there first.
Remember that if there are changes or an upset at home he may well reject the potty for a while. Learning to use the potty will give LT a real sense of achievement.

Potty training problems

If LT seems reluctant to get out of nappies, there could
be several reasons. He might be slow to train because
he's racing around so much he doesn't have time
to sit. Try encouraging boys to wee
while you hold the potty.
If he simply refuses to use
the potty, talk to your
health visitor or have him
checked by the doctor.
Potty training can become
a battleground between
LT and his parents, and
a symptom of deeper
behavioural problems.
If he's over five and still
wet during the day or night
he can be seen at a specialist
clinic (ask your GP to refer you).

Tips for the reluctant sitter

⭐ **Make sure he's not constipated** – it might be hurting him (try extra water and fruit).

⭐ **Give him a break** – try again in a few weeks.

⭐ **Make the loo interesting!** – Put posters and pictures on the walls. Have a special box of books at the right height for when he's sitting.

GOOD SLEEPING HABITS

Getting LT into good sleeping habits while he's still a baby will give him all the benefits of sound, healthy sleep, while helping you to return to civilised sleeping patterns sooner.

For more detailed advice see The Little Terror Good Sleeping Guide

The aim is:

1) to start LT off with good sleeping habits, or
2) if he's not sleeping at the right times, making changes so that
he learns to go to sleep and stay asleep when you want him to.
He obviously won't sleep through the night at first, he'll need
to wake frequently to feed, but by six months he won't need so
many feeds as he will be having solids during the day.

The secret is to teach LT from the start how to go to sleep on his
own. Then, when he wakes, he'll be able to go back to sleep by
himself. Try to cut down on the times you let him 'drop off' on
the breast, bottle or in your arms.

Once a day encourage LT to get himself to sleep by putting him down awake in his crib and rocking him, or taking him for a walk in his pram. Try singing or gently patting him to help him settle. If it doesn't work straight away don't despair! It might take a week or two for LT to be able to fall asleep on his own, but it will be very satisfying when he does. Then try it twice a day, and so on. With a bit of luck, by the time he's six months he'll be settling without too much fuss in the day and going out like a light at bedtime.

Tips for the reluctant sleeper

Some babies are more reluctant than others to settle down to sleep on their own.

☆ Check first if there are straightforward reasons for LT waking – is he too hot or too cold, ill, hungry or thirsty, or have there been any changes at home (a holiday for instance)?

☆ It's easier to teach LT how to fall asleep during the day, when you're less tired. Naps are best between 9.30am and 3.30pm so it's not too close to his usual bedtime. Normal naps won't affect how he sleeps at night.

⭐ **Stay with him until he's asleep** – using the soothing methods on page 34; it could take up to an hour to start with.

⭐ **Once he's used to settling** – instead of patting and singing, sit next to the cot with just your hand on him. Stay until he's asleep. After one week, start moving your chair away, about one foot every three days, until you are near the door. When he's settling in his cot, with you on the chair by the door, start nipping out for ten seconds at a time and then gradually increase the time you are out of the room. This might take two or three weeks, but could be quicker.

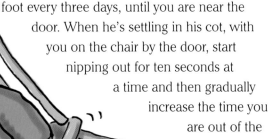

☆ Build a bedtime routine – for example, have a quiet half hour after tea before bath or wash; then give him a bottle or breastfeed in the bedroom and look at a book together; finally a cuddle and kiss goodnight and out. Use the same routine when he's older and using a bed, but leave out the milk (bad for teeth).

✩ **When LT is about six months** – reduce his night-time bottle feeds by watering down the milk gradually. If breastfed, slowly increase a period at night where you don't feed him. Pick a time when he usually has a good feed, say 11.30pm and then, for three nights, try not feeding him after that until 2.00am. For the next three nights, try not feeding him again until 2.30am. Increase the time by around half an hour every three days.

✩ Avoid letting him sleep in your bed – he could overheat, which increases the incidence of cot death. Once he's allowed in to your bed a few times, he'll think he's got rights to it and won't be too pleased if you ever deny him!

✩ If LT is ill or teething – or his routine has been upset, he'll need a lot more cuddles and you won't be able to carry out a lot of the tips above. Try again when he's better!

✩ For more advice, read *The Little Terror Good Sleeping Guide*, in this series.

✩ Get all the rest you can – use family and friends to help you.

MEALTIMES

LT's mealtimes can be great fun. There's nothing like eating together to make you feel like a family. All families have their own mealtime routines and yours will be different from The Knowitalls' and the Doneitalls'. LT will be learning from your behaviour. If you lick your plate, so will he. Set a good example – when he begins weaning, sit down and eat or drink something with him.

Most under fives go through stages of refusing to eat certain foods. This is perfectly normal and doesn't mean that LT's going to waste away. As long as it's only for a short time he won't harm himself at all. Follow the tips on pages 42-3 to establish enjoyable family mealtimes.

Mealtime tips

⭐ Make it fun – chat to LT about what you're doing.

⭐ Stick to regular mealtimes even when he's weaning – don't let him pick and snack.

⭐ Be prepared – shop in advance and prepare meals in good time so that he doesn't get too hungry waiting.

⭐ Don't make a habit of meals in front of the TV – it's OK as an occasional weekend treat, but very distracting.

Stick to regular mealtimes

☆ Never force LT to eat – even when he's weaning, you'll know when he's had enough. He'll turn his head away, push his bowl on the floor, spit his food out and make some 'I've had enough' noises.

☆ Don't reward him for refusing your nutritious meal by offering him his favourite sweet things – if he really does hate the food you've prepared, offer him a healthy alternative.

☆ Try to keep your cool – though it won't always be easy.

Eating problems

Most parents who worry about under-eating have babies who are well-fed or even overweight! If you stay calm and respond sensitively when LT refuses food, it's unlikely to become serious. If he hardly eats and regularly won't take anything at all he might just have found the ideal way to get your undivided attention. Nevertheless, if you are worried, consult you doctor or health visitor, if only to put your mind at rest.

Some feeding dos and don'ts for those with problems

DO

Encourage him to finish his meal even if he's taking ages. Try to be calm.

Put very little on his plate to start with.

Give lots of praise for even a little improvement.

Eat with him, talk to him, make it fun.

Ask his friend to tea – the one who eats like a horse.

Invite other people to lunch; it will take the focus off LT, and you'll have a social life.

DON'T

Don't force him to eat.

Don't let him get overtired.

Don't give him only what you would like him to eat (be realistic).

Don't give him snacks between meals.

Don't try to bribe him to eat with sweets and cakes (he'll soon have you round his little finger and will eat nothing else).

WHEN THINGS GO WRONG

It's the nightmare scenario: you're at the end of your tether, LT's unhappy and behaving like a monster. How could it have come to this? Things can go wrong for many reasons. Somewhere along the line, LT has learned that he gets more attention for being naughty than for being good. So naturally that's what he does. The key is to change your reaction to him so that he learns he has to change his behaviour.

Babies aren't born bad and parents are usually doing the best they can, but If LT learns that he can get what he wants by being naughty, he'll continue to behave that way. He knows he's being naughty. Believe it or not, he still wants to please you. He doesn't really want you to be cross,

he just wants your attention. However exasperated you feel, try to talk to him and really listen to what he has to say. He'll feel he's been taken notice of, and it may avoid the need for a confrontation. Read through the survival tips for difficult behaviour on page 52. Although the causes may differ, the solutions are usually the same. Also, read back over the 'Fair Rules' section (page 14).

Temper tantrums

What are they? They are a violent reaction to LT's frustrations and usually involve screaming, shouting, lying on the floor and crying; sometimes he may bang his head, kick and push others, or throw things. He's unlikely to hurt himself.

BWAAA

Why do they happen? At this age LT wants to do so much and can become frustrated by his immature skills. He wants to tell you things but can't get the words out (if he's a late developer in speech, this will be even harder) and you might have been distracted at the time he was struggling to explain something particularly important. He could have just demolished his building block tower by mistake because he was having a bad hand/eye co-ordination day. He may be jealous of a new baby and be asking for more love and attention. If Mum is busy, he learns that if he has a tantrum, he gets what he wants, i.e., attention. At least it's a response, which is better than nothing.

At what age do they happen? They can start before he's eighteen months and peak at the terrible twos. A fifth of parents of two-year-olds will be getting a double-dose each day. By the age of four, thankfully, tantrums are rare.

When do they happen? Often when LT is tired or hungry. We've all witnessed screaming, purple-faced LTs embarrassing their parents at the supermarket checkout. As a parent, this is a no-win situation. If you reason with him you're seen as too soft. If you get angry you can almost hear people thinking 'no wonder the kid behaves like that'. Meanwhile, the tantrum carries on anyway. For help in situations like these, look through the survival tips on page 52. It might save your sanity!

You might not know exactly why a tantrum occurs, but you won't be in any doubt that LT is VERY ANGRY. Put yourself in his shoes, and remind yourself how you feel when you're angry. Are you easily pacified or reasonable when you're seeing red?

LT's friends will probably range from the quiet-as-a-mouse types to full-on, raging hurricanes. At three years old, one in every ten will be very active, and difficult to manage. If LT is one of these, you'll need all the help you can get. He may have been born like it, sleeping little, yet with masses of energy, tearing around, climbing over sofas, leaving the taps running and generally getting into mischief.

A very active child is not naughty on purpose. He just can't contain his energy.

If this all sounds a bit horrific, it's not all bad news. Having a lot of energy can be a big advantage in life. Here are some things you can do to help him gain more control over his life and help you rescue yours.

SURVIVAL TIPS

Tantrums? Disobedience? Super-activity?
Whatever the cause of LT's problems, the solutions
are largely the same.

⭐ **Don't ask for trouble.** Don't go shopping when you're both irritable, it's a recipe for disaster. Plan your trip when he's not tired or hungry and you are feeling OK. Make several short trips rather than one mammoth one.

⭐ **Distraction.** The best way to stop a tantrum is to catch it before it takes hold. Work on your repertoire of distraction techniques. Point to something

and really exaggerate your interest, 'Look at that bird on the tree!' or 'Look! What a lovely worm.' You'll sound ridiculous, but if it works (and it often does!) who cares?

⭐ **Be consistent** in your own responses to LT. If you're not, you will confuse him and undermine his security. He'll also learn to exploit inconsistencies.

⭐ **Stay cool.** Try not to lose your temper or take tantrums personally. Shouting just prolongs the agony. The best response is to ignore it and either quietly do something else or go out of the room if you can. A head-on confrontation will only make things worse.

⭐ **Don't give in.** 'No' must mean precisely that. Don't bribe him with cuddles or sweets as this will teach him that tantrums pay.

⭐ **More upset than angry?** It might be worth holding him firmly, as long as you are not feeling angry yourself and can reassure LT.

⭐ **Praise the good things he does** and limit the 'nos' and 'don'ts'.

⭐ **Teach him to concentrate.** Start him off on a game and encourage him to finish it by himself with you nearby.

☆ **Look at him** and get eye contact when you talk to him. Keep instructions short and make sure he's listening.

☆ **Look after yourselves.** Give yourselves a break, even if it is only for an hour or two. Use family or friends.

☆ **Give him cuddles** as soon as he has come out of his mood, and leave the subject alone. He's likely to be upset and to need reassurance that you still love him.

☆ **Use punishment as a last resort** – see the section on discipline (page 61) and 'Time Out' (page 62).

☆ **Beware of the cycle of bad behaviour** (see pages 56-7).

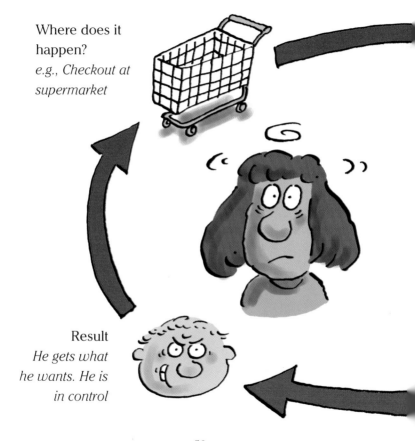

Where does it happen?
e.g., Checkout at supermarket

Result
He gets what he wants. He is in control

Cycle of bad behaviour

What does
LT do?
*Screams for
sweets*

What do you do?
*Give him sweets
to keep him quiet*

Making changes with 'Special Playtimes'

If things are going wrong, you'll both need to make changes to improve the situation. To start with, if things are really bad, you may have to teach LT *how* to play. One way is to give him back a sense of control by having a 'Special Playtime'. This is a time when LT chooses exactly what he wants to do and you join in. Try starting with just five minutes of 'Special Playtime' every day. This gives you both a good opportunity to make real progress in your relationship. LT will feel special when you focus all your attention on him. Let him choose what he wants to do, so that he feels in control. Be realistic though, and don't expect instant results. It will take a week or two before you both begin to learn to respond differently to each other.

Tips for special playtime

☆ Let LT choose what he wants to play.

☆ Ask him what he wants you to do.
He might not tell you the first few times,
so just watch him and give him
encouragement.

☆ Join in with LT's game.

☆ Repeat what he's saying, for
example if LT says 'I like my dinosaur,'
show in your response that you've
listened to his comments, for example,
'You really like your dinosaur, don't you?'

☆ Smile and look at LT.

☆ Give him a friendly touch or even a cuddle if it doesn't
interrupt the game.

☆ Ignore silly or bad behaviour.

☆ Show LT you are interested through your comments, for example, 'You're building a big tower,' or, 'Oh look, teddy's flying!'

☆ Comment on how LT's looking, for example, 'You look happy today.'

☆ Don't tell him what to do or ask questions. Don't try to teach him, or criticise him or say no to his suggestions.

☆ You want LT to be enjoying himself, so don't interrupt or try and take control.

☆ Give plenty of praise, like 'You *are* clever!' or, 'Well done, you *have* built a tall tower.'

Discipline

This is the last resort, when you have tried everything, LT is still being naughty and you feel he's setting out to make your life a misery. Of course you still love him to bits (even though sometimes it may not feel like it) but you also know you need to regain control.

Although it's tempting to shout at, or even smack LT, it would actually make matters worse. He would tend to follow your example and do the same. The first thing to do is take away whatever is the object of his bad behaviour – if he's throwing his toys about, remove them, or if he's kicking the TV, switch it off.

61

Time Out

If you've tried absolutely everything else, to no effect, introduce the 'Time Out' technique, as described here using the example of LT kicking the TV.

Tell LT not to kick the TV. If he complies, praise him and leave it at that.

If he goes straight back to kick the TV, tell him you will count up to five and if he does not obey he'll have to sit in the hall, or sit on the 'Time Out' chair. (This must have been explained to him beforehand.)

Tell LT that he's going to the chair because he has not done what you have asked him to do.

If he complies, praise him; if not take him to the 'Time Out' chair. Make him stay there for at least thirty seconds and up to two minutes.

Tell LT he can leave the 'Time Out' chair if he does not kick the TV. If he agrees not to kick it, praise him for doing what you asked and give him a cuddle.

Make it his decision

If he does not agree, repeat 'Time Out' in the same way.

If he wants to *stay* in the 'Time Out' chair for any length of time, it's not working; he may be using it to get your attention, which is rewarding him, so go to 'Special Playtime' (page 58) before trying 'Time Out' again.

Very few parents will need to go this far but, as a final attempt to change a pattern of bad behaviour, 'Time Out' can be very effective.

By working with LT you'll understand that good behaviour doesn't mean being good all the time. It's not about sitting quietly in a sailor suit, but about playing creatively and getting along with others. It's about having fun within the boundaries and sometimes testing them. All children play up at some time or other, and good luck to them! We all need a bit of spirit in this life.

If things go wrong, help LT make changes, unlearn bad ways and learn new ones. It will take time and patience but, hopefully, after a few weeks, you'll notice a marked improvement in LT's behaviour and in your relationship with him. If you find you are still not coping, your health visitor or doctor should be able to give you support or refer you to a behavioural clinic. *Good Luck!*